# Climbing Mount Kilimanjaro

## By Ned Munger

Illustrated by Eric Rowe

## DOMINIE PRESS

Pearson Learning Group

Publisher: Raymond Yuen
Project Editor: John S. F. Graham
Editor: Bob Rowland
Designer: Greg DiGenti
Illustrator: Eric Rowe

Published by:

### ꝑ Dominie Press, Inc.

1949 Kellogg Avenue
Carlsbad, California 92008 USA

www.dominie.com

1-800-232-4570

Paperback ISBN 0-7685-2069-X
Printed in Singapore
    8 9 10 V0ZF 14 13 12 11 10

# Table of Contents

Chapter One
# Anywhere in the World

**W**hen Julie was twelve and Curtis was eleven, their Uncle Bill offered to take them on a trip anywhere in the world.

Julie and Curtis looked at maps and read books about places that interested them. Then they told Uncle Bill they wanted to climb the highest mountain in Africa.

Mount Kilimanjaro, in Tanzania, is almost 20,000 feet high. That's about 3.5 miles up.

Could two young people from Los Angeles make it to the top of a mountain in Africa? According to the rules, Julie and Curtis were old enough. Another requirement was that they be healthy and physically fit, which they were.

But first they had to learn more about Tanzania. Curtis asked a smart question at dinner one night.

"Uncle Bill, I was studying the map of Africa that you gave me. There is a funny bump on the border between Kenya and Tanzania right where Mount Kilimanjaro is. Why is there a bump?"

Julie had read about it. She answered

proudly, "Silly, that's because Kilimanjaro used to be in British territory, but Kaiser Wilhelm, the ruler of Germany, wanted the highest point in Africa to be in his territory; so his cousin Victoria, the queen of England, gave it to him."

In the next few days Uncle Bill, Julie, and Curtis outfitted themselves with boots and clothing for the trip. Mornings on Kilimanjaro are frosty, so they would need warm jackets. But by midafternoon, they would be more comfortable in T-shirts under the hot equatorial sun.

They got passports and visas, shots to protect them from typhoid fever and tetanus, and pills to prevent malaria.

At last they were ready. They flew in a 747 over the Arctic Circle to London, and then over the Mediterranean Sea and the Sahara Desert to Nairobi, where they spent the night. The next day, a smaller plane took them to Moshi, a town at the base of the mountain. From Moshi, they could see the snow-capped peak they hoped to reach.

Chapter Two

# Getting Used to the Altitude

In 1848, people did not believe the first Europeans to see Kilimanjaro when they reported that there was snow at the equator. How could there be snow in such a hot place? Geographers said the white stuff must be salt deposited by the now dormant volcano. They didn't know that the higher the altitude, the colder the air, even at the equator.

As Julie, Curtis, and Uncle Bill walked around Moshi in the morning, the air was crisp. Moshi is about 4,000 feet above sea level, and they had to get used to the altitude.

Rich volcanic soil from the mountain, fed by clear streams from the glaciers, has produced magnificent coffee in the region for more than a century. Julie, Curtis, and Uncle Bill visited the nearby coffee *shamba*, or ranch, owned by Uncle Bill's friend, Hassan. During their stay, Hassan showed them how coffee is picked, dried, and then packed in *jute*, or burlap bags, for shipment to market.

In the afternoon they took a brisk walk to prepare themselves for the next day's climb. Then they rested and watched TV—a soap opera in Swahili, the main language in Tanzania.

At five the next morning, they set off for three days of climbing. There were thirteen people in their party, including a leader and three porters. The landscape changed as they climbed, slowly, in single file. In the dense forest, they saw elephant dung and black-and-white colobus monkeys.

Then they came to a broad grassy plain dotted with flowering plants. They stepped their way carefully across the stones in the many streams that coursed down the mountain. As they emerged above the tree line, they saw many stones covered with lichens and moss.

About a third of the way up, they came to a hut, where they spent the night. They slept soundly and felt refreshed as they began the second day of climbing.

## Chapter Three
# Acute Mountain Sickness

Kilimanjaro has three extinct volcanic cones. To reach the highest peak, snow-capped Kibo, you don't need expert mountaineering skills.

As Julie, Curtis, and Uncle Bill climbed, clouds passed below them. Occasionally, one wrapped them in its white fleece, and they were suddenly cold. Then the sun shone through, and they had to protect themselves from the intense ultraviolet light.

Curtis had quite a headache because of the altitude. The higher you go, the less oxygen there is in the air. It takes time for your body to adapt to the thinner air. Most of the climbers stopped every few yards to breathe deeply. They also drank frequently from the cold streams, even if they didn't feel thirsty. Dehydration—lack of water—makes it more difficult to adapt to high altitudes.

It's important to take it easy to prevent acute mountain sickness, a serious condition. If you exert yourself before your body has adapted, you can become very sick and even die. Curtis's headache

wasn't incapacitating, but Julie worried about him anyway.

Now they could see the hut where they would spend their second night. It was about 1,000 feet up the mountain, but it looked tantalizingly close. One member of the climbing party, a husky football player, passed the rest of the group, walking rapidly up toward the hut.

Julie, Curtis, and Uncle Bill climbed *poli-poli*, or *slowly*. When they reached the hut, they found the football player lying on a canvas stretcher. He had all the symptoms of acute mountain sickness.

The group leader assigned two porters to carry him down the mountain. Later, the climbers heard over the walkie-talkie that he was recovering at a lower altitude.

Julie and Curtis snuggled in their blankets around the fire while the porter cooked a dinner of hot soup, toast, and *chai* (Swahili for *tea*). After eating, the group stretched out in the cold hut, still wearing all their clothes. They slept fitfully because of the altitude.

## Chapter Four
# The Treacherous Slope

The leader woke the climbers at two in the morning. The three-quarter moon cast an eerie glow across the mountain. Even though Julie, Curtis, and Uncle Bill had slept in all of their clothes, they felt cold and stiff. It felt good to warm their hands by the fire and sip hot *chai*.

For this final day of climbing, they emptied their packs of everything except the essentials and put on their thick woolen helmets with narrow slits for the eyes and mouth. They were ready!

The black cinder path was hard to follow in the dark. And it was an exhausting surface to walk on. Three steps up. Two steps sliding down. They had been climbing for two hours, and the sun had yet to rise. Julie was afraid she couldn't go on. She began to cry. Curtis comforted her and tried to help her up the treacherous slope.

But then Curtis slipped and cut his leg on a rock. His pants had torn, and blood was oozing out of the wound. The leader asked Curtis if he could climb another 100 feet to a small cave. Curtis gritted his

teeth and nodded.

In the cave, the leader washed the wound with disinfectant, picked out little slivers of cinder, and wrapped a tight compress around Curtis's leg. Julie held Curtis's hand, and Uncle Bill tried to keep him from rolling down the slanted floor of the cave. A porter made *chai*, and Curtis rested.

To take their minds off their discomfort, Uncle Bill read to them from *The Snows of Kilimanjaro*, a story by Ernest Hemingway.

"Close to the western summit," Uncle Bill read, "there is the dried and frozen carcass of a leopard. No one has explained what the leopard was seeking at that altitude."

Julie and Curtis wondered whether they would find the leopard if they reached the top.

Chapter Five

# Reaching the Summit at Last

As Julie, Curtis, and Uncle Bill sat at the edge of the cave and watched the sun rise, their spirits rose, too. It was thrilling to see the country of Kenya on the other side of the mountain. The view extended all the way across the equator.

To the Bantu-speaking Chaga people who live on its slopes, *Kilimanjaro* means "mountain of the spirit." Could the climbers' rising spirits take them up the final cold, slippery trail to the top?

The night before, around the fire, one of the climbers speculated that maybe half of them would make it to the summit, but certainly not the children. Hearing that made Julie as mad as an eleven-year-old can get—and that was pretty mad!

But now Julie worried about all the blood that Curtis had lost. Uncle Bill offered to stay in the cave with him while Julie and the others went to the top. But Curtis would not hear of it. He was the first to stand up.

"Let's go!" he said.

The leader broke a trail in the icy

crust that had formed overnight. Again, the climbers fought gravity, taking three steps up and sliding two steps back.

At last—despite the predictions—the whole party reached the summit. Looking over the crater's rim, they saw many fumaroles, or vents in the volcanic rock, releasing smoke several hundred feet into the air. In the other direction, far below, lay all of Africa.

Julie and Curtis made snowballs from a drift and threw them as far as they could, hoping they would reach the equator, however unlikely that was. (The equator was more than 150 miles away!) They may not have been the only eleven- and twelve-year-olds to reach the top of Kilimanjaro, but they must be among the special few, and certainly the first brother-and-sister team from Los Angeles.

To mark the achievement, the porters crowned them with wreaths of everlasting flowers.

Curtis said that everyone should get a chance to climb Mount Kilimanjaro. The leader of the party explained that the snow cap has decreased 75 percent over the past 100 years and may be gone by the year 2015. The mountain will never be the same sight after that happens.

They never found the frozen leopard carcass. Did it ever really exist? Julie, Curtis, and Uncle Bill thought so. But it didn't really matter—the climb was its own reward.